ANABEL Doesn't Talk

Amanda Johnson

Illustrations by Blueberry Illustrations

© 2016 Amanda Johnson
All rights reserved. No part of this publication may be reproduced, distributed, or transmitted in any form or by any means, including photocopying, recording, or other electronic or mechanical methods, without the prior written permission of the publisher.

ISBN- 13: 978-1541243316

I like to say hello to people when they approach me and goodbye when they leave.

But Mommy and Daddy tell me I shouldn't say hello and goodbye to everyone. They say I shouldn't talk to strangers.

A stranger is anybody you don't know.

There are all kinds of strangers and it's a good idea to know when I can talk to one.

There are strangers that I've never met before, like the people we pass by in the store.

These are the strangers I shouldn't talk to.

Some strangers I've seen before and have even spoken to. Like Mr. Henry, he lives down the street and walks his dog past our house every day.

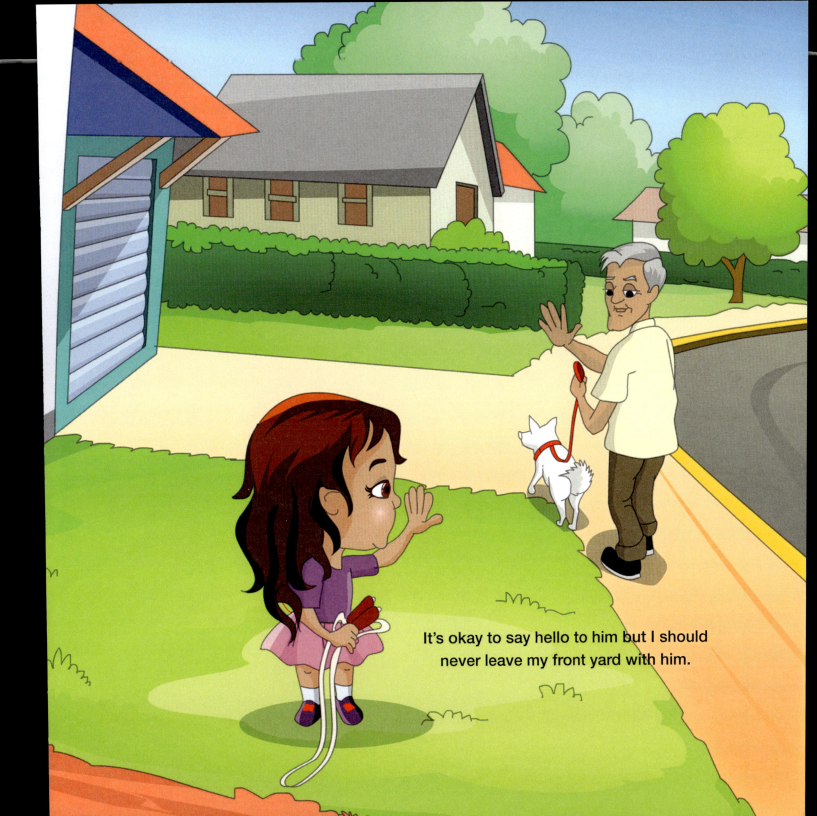
It's okay to say hello to him but I should never leave my front yard with him.

And there are some strangers that I've never met before but are safe and can even help me if I'm lost or scared.

Like a police officer.

Or a lifeguard at the beach.

Well, if I go to the park with my babysitter and someone asks me if I'd like to see their puppy, I should always say "No, I don't talk to strangers" and quickly find my babysitter.

If I can't find her, I should look for a store employee. A store employee is someone who works in the store. She will usually be wearing a uniform with a name tag. I can tell her I'm lost and need help finding my mommy.

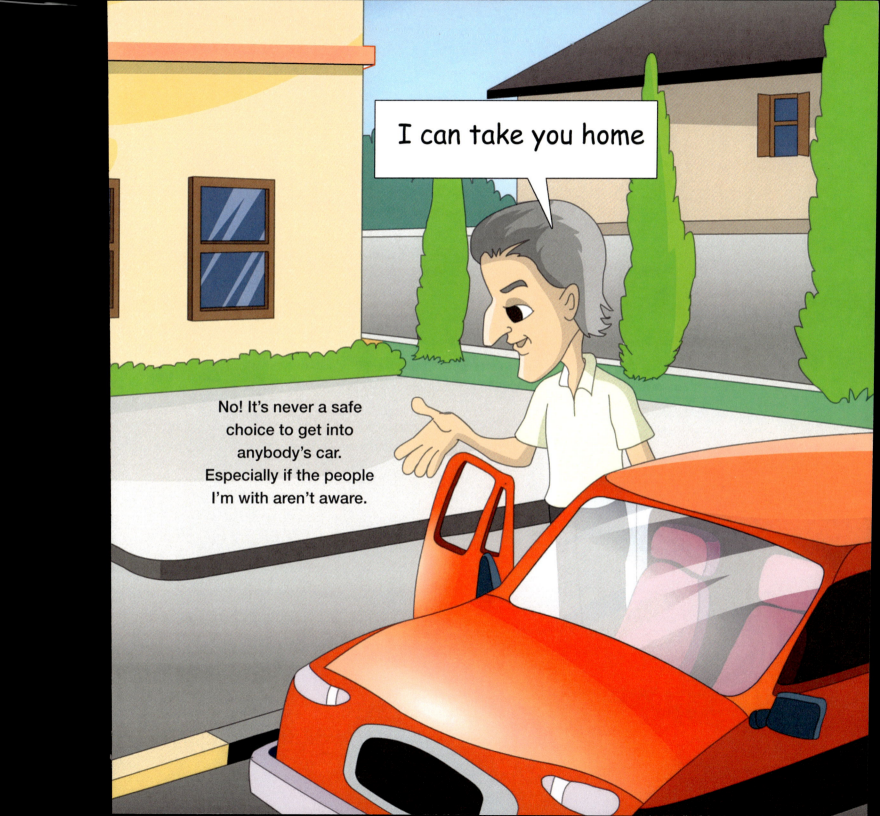

Also, whenever a stranger tries to talk to me it's important to tell the person I'm with exactly what happened.

My Mommy, Daddy, Grandma, or babysitter should always be aware of what's happening around me for my own safety.

Talking to strangers is not always a safe thing to do. Therefore I don't say hello to everyone I meet, even though I would like to.

And I make sure to stay close to the person taking care of me so that strangers don't approach me.

The End

Made in the USA
Lexington, KY
01 September 2018